BRITAIN
~AN AERIAL VIEW~

Designed by Sally Strugnell

2727
This 1991 edition published by Coombe Books
© 1991 Coombe Books
Printed and bound in Hong Kong
ISBN 0 86283 849 5

BRITAIN
~AN AERIAL VIEW~

COOMBE BOOKS

Redolent with memories of the martyrdom of Thomas à
Becket, the medieval richness of Canterbury is
summarised in the soaring stateliness of the cathedral,
whose magnificent architecture ranges from Norman to
Perpendicular, and whose 13th-century stained glass is
the equal of Bourges and Chartres.

In the days when the Roman legions, with all their might and power, straddled this land, through present day England, Wales and parts of Scotland, they called the portion of the island they occupied *Britannia*, and the name they gave has come down through the ages.

England, the home of the Mother of Parliaments, and William Blake's "green and pleasant land", has a wealth of scenery to delight the eye. There are the mountains and tarns of the Lake District; the windswept moors of the Pennines; the rolling Yorkshire Dales; the sleepy Cotswold villages, unchanged with time; the warm seashores of Cornwall, washed by the Gulf Stream; the bustling capital of London with the mighty River Thames flowing through its heart; prehistoric Stonehenge standing on the sweep of Salisbury Plain; historic towns and cities like Canterbury, Salisbury and York; the cries of birds echoing over the desolate Fens of East Anglia; farmers ploughing their hedgerow-lined fields, and dry-stone walls which march over the uplands; the great, craggy landscpaes of the northern counties, and the seemingly endless moors of the southwest.

The immense variety of vistas almost seems to take the traveller unawares. Who would think that this relatively small country could contain such diversity? Leave behind the busy thoroughfares of any crowded town and you can see the undulating countryside before you; golden corn sways in the summer breezes under a blue sky containing ever-changing patterns of clouds; dense copses of trees stand silent with the weight of years; in springtime lambs dance in their sprightly fashion in lush green fields; rivers and streams wend their ways to the sea, which is sometimes calm and restful, but often displays the fierce force of turbulent nature as waves pound the nation's sea-girt walls. John Keats so well expressed his feelings for the land of his birth:

> *Happy is England! I could be content*
> *To see no other verdure than its own;*
> *To feel no other breezes than are blown*
> *Through its tall woods with high romances blent.*

Scotland is a majestic country of rugged beauty; its turbulent history reflecting its people's fight to maintain their clan heritage and identity. For Sir Walter Scott it was the:

> *Land of brown heath and shaggy wood;*
> *Land of the mountain and the flood!*

It is also a country of jewel-like lochs; towering, scented conifers; bracken-covered moors; ice-cool streams that go to the making of the finest malt whiskies; castle strongholds; golf courses of international renown and a special kind of people. The landscapes are of a particularly wild and natural beauty, interwoven with a melancholic sense of history and strife. There have been heroes made of such men as Robert the Bruce and Sir William Wallace, both doughty fighters against the Sassenachs. There were bloody battles fought, particularly at Bannockburn and Culloden, and there was defeat when the Scottish came south to Flodden Field:

> *Dool and wae for the order, sent our lads to the Border!*
> *The English, for ance, by guile wan the day;*
> *The Flowers of the Forest, that fought aye the foremost,*
> *The prime of our land, are cauld in the clay.* (Jean Elliot)

There are still many places in Scotland that have not been changed by the hand of time – Glencoe broods with an air of menace where the Macdonalds were slain by their treacherous guests.

The islands dotted around its coasts are places of enchantment, repositories of ancient culture and myth. It is a proud nation, having known hardship and injustice as well as prosperous times.

Wales is a mountainous country, divided by beautiful valleys, a land of crystal streams, and rivers including the Severn, Clwyd, Conway and Usk. It is blessed with wonderful scenery along the rugged Pembrokeshire coast, in the magnificent Snowdonia National Park andthe glacier-scoured hills of the Brecon Beacons. It is a land of legend, where the stories tell of King Arthur's wizard, Merlin, living in his crystal cave. He was the child of a wizard and a princess, gifted with prophecy, becoming a prominent personage at the court of King Arthur, where his immense knowledge was much sought after. Wales is also a country which has produced great singers and fine poets, such as Dylan Thomas:

> *All the sun long it was running, it was lovely, the hay-*
> *Fields high as the house, the tunes from the chimneys, it was air*
> *And playing, lovely and watery*
> *And fire green as grass.*

Much of the varied and historic attractions of Britain lie around the next corner! It was J.B.Priestley who said that, "it would not surprise me if somebody decided to follow some tiny overgrown lane and then found that at the end of it Camelot was still there, with nettles thick around a dusty Round Table."

The Isles of Scilly lie to the west of Cape Cornwall, near the fabled lost land of Lyonesse. Of the cluster of islands, that of St Martins (facing page) is one of the largest.

St Ives (right), in Cornwall, has been a magnet for artists since the 1880s, when painters were lured here by the attraction of its crisp, clear light. The most highly regarded part of the town lies on the neck of land between the harbour and the surfing beach of Porthmeor. The streets are narrow, and galleries founded by the artist community are to be found in the steep alleys.

Close by the Devon border, where the River Tamar marks
the boundary between Cornwall and the rest of
England, runs the most dramatic seascape walk in Britain.
The coastal path commences at Mount Edgcumbe
Country Park in the south, runs westward to round
Land's End (below) and Gwennap Head (left), and
then continues its way up the Atlantic seaboard, to
finish at Bude.

Lying to the south of St Ives, Cornwall, is St Michael's Mount (above). This lofty, isolated mass of rock, some twenty-one acres in extent, is crowned by the most romantically-sited of all medieval castles. At high water St Michael's Mount is separated from the mainland by a stretch of water, but at low tide a cobblestone causeway connects the two.

Newquay (left) is the largest and most popular holiday resort in Cornwall. It lies on the county's northern coast, midway between Land's End and Bude. Once it was merely a fishing hamlet, and was virtually unknown other than for its pilchard catch. The fish came periodically, and it was the job of the *huer* – who occupied Huer's House, on the headland, and from whom we get the expression 'hue and cry' – to watch for the shoals reddening the water, at which time, with a great shout he alerted the villagers. Sunshine reflects on the wind-blown Helford River, at Cornwall's Porth Navas (facing page).

The South West Peninsula Coastal Path passes enchanting places, such as Pentire Head (below), where in spring the headland grass is carpeted with wild flowers – blue squills, primrose, bloody cranesbill, sea pink and mesembryathimum – and the sheer cliff face becomes the nesting ground of shag and cormorant.

Coverack in Cornwall is a typical fishing village, complete with stone-built, whitewashed cottages, a miniature, classically-shaped harbour and a lifeboat station. Coverack is noted for the heroism of its lifeboat crews, who have, many times, set out to rescue those wrecked on the forbidding Manacles, just three miles away.

The harbour (left) at Polperro, Cornwall, is but three acres in extent, and dry at low tide, with so narrow an entrance that it can be barred against winter storms by horizontal baulks of timber being dropped into slots in the masonry.

Longships Lighthouse (facing page top) may present a tranquil scene, with sunshine reflected on the calm sea, but in severe storms waves have been known to lash the 110ft-high lantern.

The ancient Cornish port of Padstow (facing page bottom), on the Camel Estuary, developed into a shipbuilding port of some importance, but steam power gradually replaced the old Padstow schooners.

By reason of their relative inaccessibility, the picturesque
Cornish coves of Talland Bay (above) and Cadgwith
(left) are among the lesser-known of the Duchy's
delights. The former has been the scene of many wrecks
over the years, and the latter is reached down a
narrow, winding lane that opens suddenly to reveal
the small cove. Cadgwith lies at the mouth of a
well-wooded valley, and the compact little village
of thatched, stone-built cottages – seemingly untouched
by the passage of time – is tucked neatly between
high, rugged cliffs. Two small beaches are
separated by 'The Todden', a diminutive headland
leading to a secluded natural bathing pool hidden
among the rocks.

Devon and the sea are inextricably linked, and her sons: Grenville, Drake, Frobisher, Fortescue, Hawkins, Chichester and Courtenay – names that loom large on the tapestry of English naval history – have for centuries braved the treacherous waters and fast-flowing tides of her headlands and shore. It is in this proud tradition that the major port of Dartmouth (above) holds fiercely to its seafaring heritage.

The rich agricultural land of the region provided the tithes to build the glorious cathedral (facing page) at Exeter. Begun in about 1275, the present cathedral is in the Decorated style, but with twin Norman towers. Exeter is a fine example of a historic English town, gradually developing over the years, from an ancient Dumnonii stronghold to the Roman Isca Dumnoniorum, to the present cathedral city.

No ancient town of England has preserved its medieval atmosphere to the same degree as has Wells, in Somerset. It takes as its centrepiece the soaring cathedral, whose renowned West Front is the most ornate of any in the country, and which displays the most extensive medieval sculpture to have survived the Reformation. Wells possesses a fine example of a medieval close, surrounded by the houses of cathedral dignitaries.

Bristol (left), in Avon, has been a port for eight hundred years, importing wine from the Angevin territory of Bordeaux and from Spain since the Middle Ages, and has traded with the New World since the 17th century. The city's medieval churches speak of its prosperity, and include St Mary Redcliffe, one of the largest parish churches in the country. The city's impressive 18th-century Corn Exchange still displays the original 'nails' upon which merchants once put their payments for goods. It is from this custom that the saying 'cash on the nail' originates.

Scanning the Bristol horizon to the east, the heavy limestone pylons of the Clifton Suspension Bridge (above) come into view. Built by that renowned bridge builder Isambard Kingdom Brunel in 1864, the structure is a powerful example of an all-too-rare phenomenon: the enhancement of nature by a man-made structure.

The city of Bath (above), in Avon, includes at its splendid Georgian heart the grandiloquence of the Palladian theme expressed to perfection in the curving terrace of John Wood the Younger's monumental Royal Circus and Crescent. Bath is the most elegant city in England, made famous by its Roman history and fashionable by the dandy, Beau Nash, in the 18th century. The Roman Baths are, of course, one of the city's main attractions and they still provide half a million gallons of water each day, at a constant temperature of 49°C.

Seeming frail and delicate in the golden light of a low sun, the Severn Bridge (right), opened in 1966, has a main span of no less than 3,240 feet, and is supported on two 400-foot-high towers.

At Stourhead (facing page), in Wiltshire, the English landscape garden of the early 18th century may be said to have been invented. It is the first of the completely informal landscape compositions which were the special English contribution to the art of gardening. At the centre of Stourhead's three-armed lake, the Doric Temple of Flora reflects its Tuscan portico in the smooth waters at its feet, and nearby can be seen the Pantheon, shining against its luxuriant, wooded background. High above the surface of the lake, amid dense trees, is the circular Temple of the Sun, after the original at Baalbek.

The broad High Street of Marlborough (right), with its fine churches at either end, has changed little over the past century.

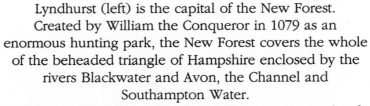

Lyndhurst (left) is the capital of the New Forest.
Created by William the Conqueror in 1079 as an
enormous hunting park, the New Forest covers the whole
of the beheaded triangle of Hampshire enclosed by the
rivers Blackwater and Avon, the Channel and
Southampton Water.
To the north of Hampshire lies the quiet countryside of
Berkshire. The River Thames forms the county's northern
border, and here there are orchards extending for several
miles to the south until the Downs are reached. At
Sonning (below), a lovely riverside village with an old
mill and an eleven-arch bridge, one of the oldest
spanning the Thames, the beech woods of the heights
descend to the river's bank.

Palace House, at Beaulieu (above), in Hampshire, presently the home of Lord Montagu, once served as the gatehouse to the Cistercian abbey, now in ruins. The abbey was founded in 1204 and was at one time one of the country's most important monasteries, until the Dissolution caused its downfall. Many thousands of visitors come to Beaulieu each year to view the fascinating exhibits in the National Motor Museum.

Situated at the edge of the New Forest, Lymington (facing page), its harbour now crowded with pleasure craft, was once a thriving shipbuilding centre and, indeed, in the 14th century it supplied a considerable number of ships for the invasion of France, more even than Portsmouth.

Lymington is a small, pleasant town with local associations with the celebrated author Edward Gibbon, who was at one time its parliamentary representative.

Of all England's counties, Sussex is the easiest to visualise. It lies in four more or less parallel strips, the northern boundary being forest, the next strip the clay weald, then the green line of the Downs, whose rolling, whaleback quality is exemplified at Storrington (left). The final zone comprises the coastline of chalk cliff and low-lying plain.

The streams that flow from the South Downs, though small, have historic importance. Rye (facing page), one of the old Cinque Ports, at one time stood at the mouth of its stream, but now, because of the receding sea, it finds itself inland. In medieval times the sea lapped at the foot of the Ypres Tower, but now the tide breaks some two miles to the south.

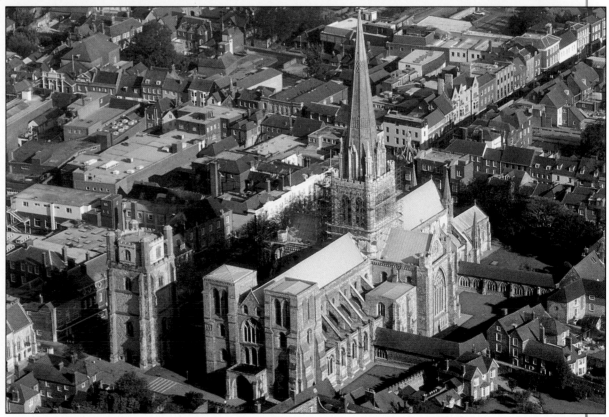

At Bodiam (facing page), Sussex, a special licence from the Crown enabled Sir Edward Dalyngrigge to build, in 1385, one of the last of the genuine medieval castles, to protect his estate from the incursions of the French. The moat, which is fed by a tributary of the River Rother, is still well filled, and together with the gatehouse, walls and drum-towers at the angles, forms one of the most beautiful and evocative castle remains in Britain. Arundel Castle (above), beside the Arun, was built to defend the break made by that river through the chalky landscape of the Downs.

Chichester, the county town of West Sussex, was known to the Romans as *Noviomagus* and their town layout – four main streets enclosed by a wall – still exists. Chichester is chiefly noted for its Georgian architecture, its fine town houses and cruciform cathedral (right). The latter is substantially the church erected over eight hundred years ago by Ralph Luffa, Bishop from 1091 until 1123. The detached bell tower beside the Great West Front is the only such example to be found in England.

34

At Scotney in Kent is to be found the happy combination of a landscape of great natural beauty, historic interest, and the rarest harmony of buildings, trees and flowers. Terraces of rhododendrons and azaleas fall sharply away from the new house to the almost unbelievably picturesque setting for the medieval castle ruins (below) that rise from the crystal waters of a lily-covered lake. The Tudor brickwork of Sissinghurst Castle (right) has mellowed to a rich, purplish red, and its confused tangle of buildings, with an unusually tall gatehouse, forms a fine backdrop for the gardens created by the author Victoria Sackville-West. It was she, and her husband Sir Harold Nicholson, who restored the once great manor house and established one of the finest gardens in the country – much of it laid out in Elizabethan style. Of particular interest is the 'white garden', planted entirely with silver-leaved white flowering species, separated by box hedges.

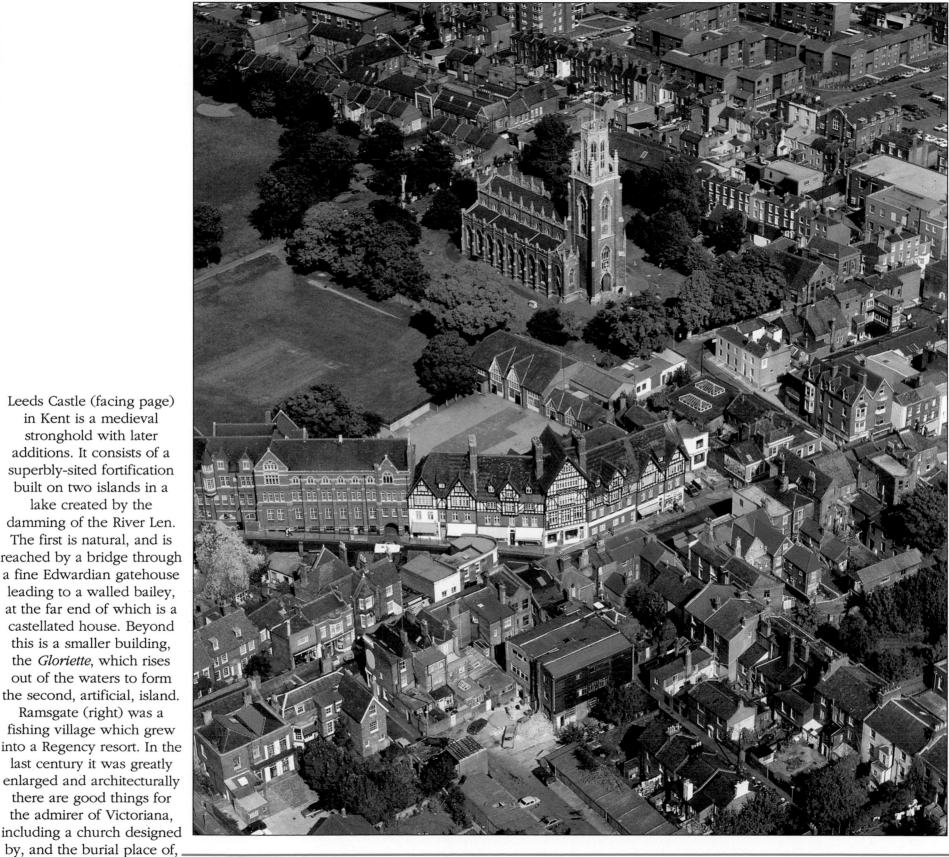

Leeds Castle (facing page) in Kent is a medieval stronghold with later additions. It consists of a superbly-sited fortification built on two islands in a lake created by the damming of the River Len. The first is natural, and is reached by a bridge through a fine Edwardian gatehouse leading to a walled bailey, at the far end of which is a castellated house. Beyond this is a smaller building, the *Gloriette*, which rises out of the waters to form the second, artificial, island. Ramsgate (right) was a fishing village which grew into a Regency resort. In the last century it was greatly enlarged and architecturally there are good things for the admirer of Victoriana, including a church designed by, and the burial place of, Augustus Pugin.

Penshurst (left) is a Wealden village that possesses a Renaissance palace, Penshurst Place. The Tudor palace does not dominate the village as it might, but sits discreetly behind the main street, to be seen on entering or leaving the village, yet never intruding on the scene of modest old houses, an inn and a well-proportioned church. Cranbrook (facing page top) was raised during the zenith of the cloth trade, towards the end of the 15th century. Hever Castle (facing page bottom) has associations with King Henry VIII, for it was here that he patiently courted and eventually won the hand of Anne Boleyn, the ill-fated mother of Elizabeth I.

A light scattering of snow serves to highlight the formal elegance of Polesden Lacey (below), set in the Surrey landscape. In such terrain, amid the county's timbered cottages and Victorian villas, with their well-tended gardens, are scattered Surrey's handful of old and precious towns: Guildford, Dorking, Farnham, Bletchingley and Reigate (left). The latter, although not mentioned by name until the 12th century, was a manor of the powerful de Warenne family, Earls of Surrey in the reign of William the Conqueror.

An atmosphere of calm pervades at Chelsea (left), born of shady, tree-lined streets, abounding in antiquities and memories of great men. For centuries the area has been secluded from the spread of London by the natural barrier of creeks running north from the Thames – where now stands Victoria Station – and by the marshy area of the Five Fields.

On the north bank of the River Thames stands the enormous neo-Gothic form of the Palace of Westminster (right), cheek by jowl with Westminster Hall. The latter was originally raised by William Rufus and altered by Richard II, who feasted ten thousand of London's poor there daily during the Christmastide of 1398. Westminster Hall has since been the scene of some of the most famous trials in England's history.

On the north bank of the grey ribbon of the Thames, which threads its course past sprawling Victorian wharves, stands London's medieval heart (left), which now constitutes that richest part of the capital known simply as The City. On its eastern boundary stands the sombre prospect of The Tower of London, a grey, uneven maze, harsh in the texture of its stone, rugged with crenellations, and dark with sinister association. Raised in brick – and among the first of its genre – is Wolsey's great palace of Hampton Court (above). Despite the influence of its great founder, however, it is Henry VIII whose image seems indelibly stamped upon the place. The view from the air reveals the vastness of the various ranges of buildings, and the formal splendour of the palace gardens – the tiltyard, the maze, the fountain garden, the sunken arbours, the knot garden and the meticulously planned and planted 'wilderness'.

In the top northeastern corner of Essex, above the Naze, the port of Harwich (left) shares the fate of many ports of departure in that it is neglected by those who visit it only to leave. Few know it as a tightly-planned medieval town with one of the earliest lighthouses in Britain – looking rather like an Eastern pagoda – and a subject, on more than one occasion, for the artist John Constable. Finchingfield (facing page) is the finest of the picturesque Essex villages. Its duckpond – at the very centre of the village, where four roads meet – fed by the River Pant; its Georgian, white-painted cottages; its gabled, barge-board houses; its 15th-century guildhall and almshouses; its church of St John the Baptist crowning the curve of the hill, all give Finchingfield an air of having just materialised from a children's storybook.

Two of East Anglia's most influential ports are Felixstowe (facing page top) and King's Lynn (right). Felixstowe occupies a sheltered position on the Suffolk coast, made fashionable by Edwardian society. Today, its docklands are an important tanker and car-ferry terminal. At King's Lynn, in neighbouring Norfolk, modern wharves jostle with the warehouses of Hanseatic traders and wool staplers for quayside frontage.

Some six miles to the north of King's Lynn is Sandringham House (facing page bottom), the private country residence of the Royal Family. It was built by Edward VII, when he was Prince of Wales, in 1867-70 and comprises a 7,000-acre estate, embracing the woodland and farmsteads of no less than seven parishes.

Norwich (left), in Norfolk, is still a rural capital; a
medieval town which is really an amalgam of
villages clinging to their old country names –
St Miles Coslany, St John's Timberhill, St Clement's-at-the-
Fye-Bridge, St James-in-Pockthorpe – each clustered
about its parish church.
The earthworks at Castle Rising (above), upon which the
Norman motte and bailey castle was superimposed, are
some of the most spectacular in England, and their scale
can only be fully appreciated from the air.

Cambridge (these pages) in Cambridgeshire is held within a softening landscape of rolling chalk hills watered by tiny streams. The town is often compared to Oxford, yet the two have few similarities and depend for their beauty on quite different circumstances. Oxford is a great city in which the university buildings stand out from the rest of the town. Cambridge, on the other hand, is a small city in which the university buildings and the churches seem to form the greater part. Among Cambridge's many treasures, its greatest is surely the Perpendicular chapel of King's College, with its fan-vaulted ceiling, and its elegant lawns running down to the willow-shrouded banks of the Cam.

In the north of Cambridgeshire, Ely (facing page) has a cathedral whose soaring western tower and octagon are visible for miles around, its stonework and white roof shining out against the dark, alluvial soil of the Fens, across wide fields of sweet grazing and root crops, where dykes cut as straight as the flight of an arrow.

The dissolution of the monasteries fostered the development of the English country house as we know it today; most landed estates include former ecclesiastic property and, indeed, the names and courtyard plans of some great classical houses – such as Woburn Abbey (below) – hark back to long-vanished cloisters.

Henley (above) is set in the beautiful wooded countryside of Oxfordshire, in the Thames Valley. The lovely old bridge, which separates the county from its neighbour, Buckinghamshire, was designed by William Hayward in 1786, and is decorated with masks of Father Thames and the goddess Isis.

Oxfordshire is the county for lovers of noble architecture. Its churches stand out as among the finest in all the shires, and its manor houses, too, represent every style of architecture, from Vanburgh's monumental Blenheim Palace to the gentle, Elizabethan brick of Mapledurham House (facing page).

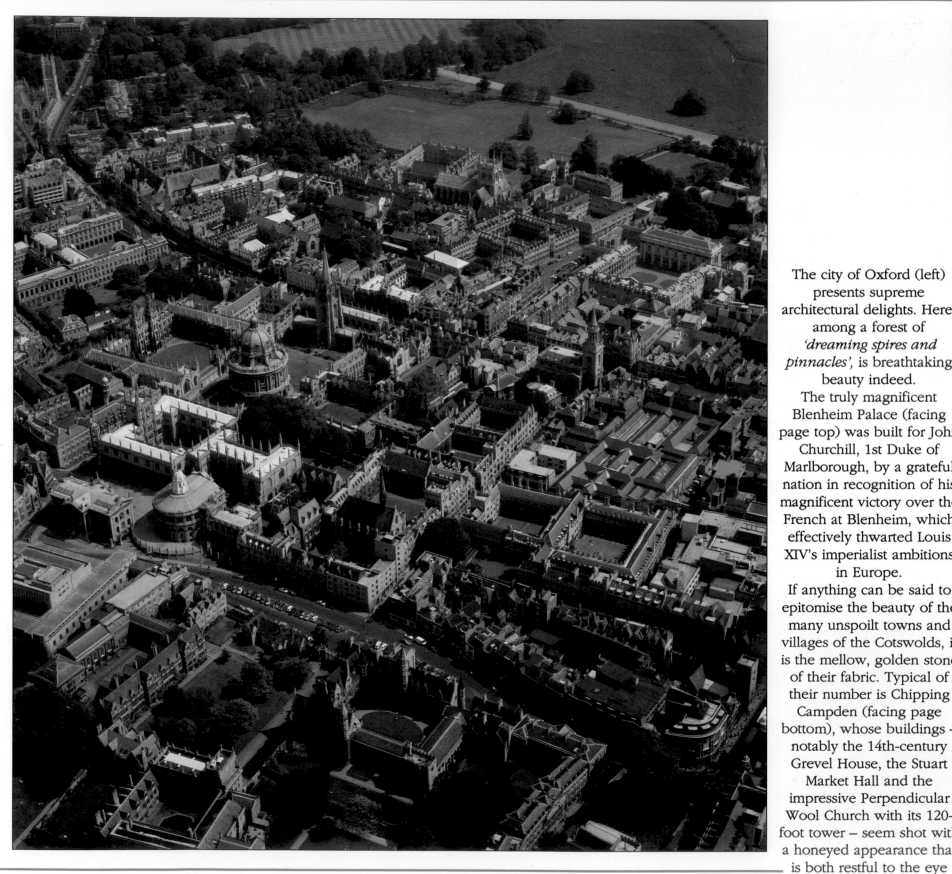

The city of Oxford (left) presents supreme architectural delights. Here, among a forest of *'dreaming spires and pinnacles'*, is breathtaking beauty indeed.

The truly magnificent Blenheim Palace (facing page top) was built for John Churchill, 1st Duke of Marlborough, by a grateful nation in recognition of his magnificent victory over the French at Blenheim, which effectively thwarted Louis XIV's imperialist ambitions in Europe.

If anything can be said to epitomise the beauty of the many unspoilt towns and villages of the Cotswolds, it is the mellow, golden stone of their fabric. Typical of their number is Chipping Campden (facing page bottom), whose buildings – notably the 14th-century Grevel House, the Stuart Market Hall and the impressive Perpendicular Wool Church with its 120-foot tower – seem shot with a honeyed appearance that is both restful to the eye and uplifting to the spirit.

Gerard Manley Hopkins saw Gloucestershire as a '…
Landscape plotted and pieced – fold, fallow and plough
….' It divides into three parts: the country of the hill, the
country of the valley and the country of the forest – three
parallel divisions extending from north to south.
The vale of the Severn is a gracious countryside, with a
red soil merging into black, where wheat flourishes and
cattle pastures and meadows are blessed with heaven's
bounty. Within this valley the Severn is a river of
infinite delights; little more than a wide stream as it
flows through Tewkesbury (below), yet ever widening as
it advances southwards to merge with the Wye and
the Bristol Channel.

From the air the old county of Worcestershire appears as a great basin, open to the south, but surrounded on its other three sides by prominent ranges of hills. From the beacon above Great Malvern (facing page) the prospect is eastward over half the Midlands and westward over the Welsh hills to the Wye Valley. The cathedral of Worcester (right) is, as it were, the coping stone that adds yet greater distinction to a very distinguished shire. In this splendid edifice is represented every style of church architecture, from early Norman to the Perpendicular. The crypt is solidly Romanesque, the choir has all the grace that the 13th century could contrive and the nave clearly belongs to the florid Decorated style. To the late 15th century is ascribed the fan-vaulted chantry chapel raised above the tomb of Prince Arthur.

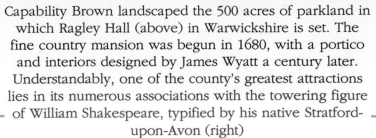

Capability Brown landscaped the 500 acres of parkland in
which Ragley Hall (above) in Warwickshire is set. The
fine country mansion was begun in 1680, with a portico
and interiors designed by James Wyatt a century later.
Understandably, one of the county's greatest attractions
lies in its numerous associations with the towering figure
of William Shakespeare, typified by his native Stratford-
upon-Avon (right)

Cardiff (left) has grown, in little more than 150 years, from a sizeable village to become the capital of the Principality of Wales, a major seaport and a university city. The area northwest of the Welsh capital, the Rhondda Valley (facing page top), was the heartland of Welsh mining and, to a very large extent, the coal from its pits was the reason for Cardiff's meteoric rise to prominence in the 19th century. Caerphilly Castle (facing page bottom) is one of the most splendid examples of military architecture in Wales. Its greatest triumph, however, is the brilliantly-conceived water defences, designed to keep out of range the deadly military catapults which, at short distance, could batter down the most robust of castle walls.

The town of Pembroke (facing page) is built on a ridge which culminates in a great mass of limestone rock. Upon this rock was built Pembroke Castle, a key fortress in the Norman settlement of Wales. In 1457 Henry Tudor, Earl of Richmond, who as Henry VII became Britain's first Tudor monarch, was born at Pembroke, and his special attachment to the town led to its close associations with royalty. There is majesty also where the land meets the sea, and the cliffs tumble down to meet the waters of the Atlantic, whose unpredictable moods have caused many ships to come to grief, as at Solva (right), not far from Pembroke.

Tenby (below) is a bright, clean-looking resort, now one of the most popular holiday towns in Wales. It is sited on a narrow limestone promontory on the western side of Carmarthen Bay. At the seaward end of the headland is the insular knoll of Castle Hill, with its ruins and its lifeboat station.

Aberystwyth (facing page) is a seat of governance as well as a holiday resort. The town grew to real importance with the establishment of its Norman castle by Edmund Crouchback in 1277. Opposite the ruins is a Victorian hotel bought a century ago to form the nucleus of the University of Wales.

Anglesey is connected to the mainland by two famous bridges: Robert Stephenson's Britannia Bridge carrying the railway, and Thomas Telford's Menai Suspension Bridge (facing page top), which has carried the road from London to Holyhead since 1826. Telford's bridge is his most famous and influential work, and is of cast iron supported by sixteen wrought-iron chains passing over tall masonry towers on either bank, each chain anchored below ground.

Of all Edward I's military constructions, it is Harlech Castle (facing page bottom) that has the most impressive setting.

The huge expanse of water (right) is held at bay by the equally impressive structure of the Claerwen Dam, in the Elan Valley.

Under the yoke of Plantagenet kings the flower of Celtic
independence retreated into the fastness of the
Snowdonia landscape, with its huge mountains, notched
in places like battlemented towers, high passes and
craggy peaks, such as the summit of Tryfan (left).
The cold, green swell of the Atlantic breaks ceaselessly
against the tiny islet of South Stack (above) and its
lighthouse of 1809.

At Rhuddlan Castle (below) King Edward I organised his administration of Wales, secure behind its massive twin gatehouses and curtain walls enclosed by a moat. The year 1282 saw not only the castle's completion, but also the diverting and canalizing of the River Clwyd.

A courageous feat of engineering led to the construction of Holyhead Harbour (facing page), whose refuge – a one-and-a-half-mile-long, solid masonry breakwater – is the result of twenty-eight years incessant labour. The port is today a major terminal for ferries to Ireland.

No one looking at the view of Lincoln (left) can fail to be struck by the dominant position of the cathedral on its high ridge above the town and encircling fenlands of the Witham Valley. The exquisitely pale colour of the beautiful Ancaster and Lincoln limestone in which the cathedral is raised is a splendid foil to the pantiles of the secular buildings which huddle around its massive bulk; reminders of the trading connections between England and Flanders which first brought pantile roofing to the eastern districts during the 17th century.

Accented by shadows cast by a low sun, mile upon mile of Lincolnshire's flat fenland countryside (right) lies divided into long, straight fields of multiple colours.

Boston (left) stands inland from the sea and is connected to the grey waters of the Wash by the River Witham as it flows down through the Great Lincolnshire Levels. By 1204, when King John granted a charter to Boston, its fame as a port was second only to that of London, and by the end of the 13th century it was paying more than the capital in customs duties. The great church at its heart, St Botolph's, is one of the largest and, in some respects, the grandest of all the parish churches in England. Almost entirely 14th century, it is an unrivalled example of late-Decorated architecture. At Ladybower Reservoir (facing page) the russet of the bracken-covered limestone peaks is relieved by milder shades of green in the vale below.

Positioned within the lovely moorland countryside of the Peaks, the spa town of Buxton (above) is the highest in the kingdom. It is sheltered by hills even higher than its 1,007ft site, nonetheless it offers gentle scenery more typical of the lowlands alongside sedate reaches of the lovely River Wye

The Romans knew Chester (facing page), where local red sandstone gives the city its distinctive hue, as *Deva*, and in the Middle Ages it was completely encircled by a two-mile stretch of walling. Chester's famous half-timbered houses, known as 'The Rows', also date from medieval times, and are unique in Europe today.

The twin-towered Minster at Beverley (facing page) is still very much the focal point of the old East Riding of Yorkshire – now officially incorporated in Humberside – and it is acknowledged as one of Europe's finest examples of ecclesiastical architecture. Within the Minster is the Percy tomb, a richly-decorated shrine to the great local land-owning family.

Nearby Selby has the equally renowned Benedictine Abbey (right), which celebrated its 900th anniversary in 1969. The town also has another claim to fame, as it is thought to be the birthplace of Henry I, the only son of William the Conqueror to be born in England.

Within the old borders of Yorkshire, now three counties, is a wealth of outstanding and diversified beauty; of bleak gritstone fells thrown into contrast against long, lovely dales; of colliery towns – that feed the power stations of Drax, Eggborough, and Ferrybridge (above) – contrasting with the Roman origin, as *Eboracum*, and the medieval heritage, of York (right), which has at its heart that *'jewel of light and glass'* the High Minster.

Lakeland, filled with the souls of her poets, is a landscape where atmosphere paints its own unique images upon the scene. The glass-like reflections of the lakes themselves are the most enigmatic, where *'Nought wakens or disturbs their tranquil tides, Nought but the char that for the may-fly leaps and breaks the mirror of the circling deep'*. The surface of lakes such as Ullswater (above) possess a piercing sheen that is not a reflection of the sky, although it may be enhanced by it, just as it is changed and patterned by every breath of wind.

Buttermere lies below High Crag (left), and here, with snow on the ancient rocks, and sculptured, marble-like cliffs gathered on all sides, the landscape comes close to the primeval state of glacial desolation.

Set like a jewel in the snow-dusted and cloud-touched landscape, Wast Water (facing page) shines beyond the east ridge of Pillar Fell.

It is the archaic setting of low, habitable dale, set against the fierce magnitude of mountain scenery, as at Ullswater (facing page), which gives the English Lakes their wistful appeal. There is never a season, whether it be springtime's unfolding or the harsh depths of winter, when the land does not offer up treasures.

The heavily-indented and thickly-wooded shoreline of Derwent Water (above) lies tranquil under a late, hazy sun. The lake's islands hold such varied interests as the remnants of the cell of St Herbert, the ruined manor of the Earl of Derwentwater and the presumed site of Arthur Ransome's Wildcat Island.

Sullen and soiled in parts, Tyne and Wear still contains Britain's finest industrial city, the former provincial capital, Newcastle (left). The Romans decided to define the western limit of their empire by constructing Hadrian's Wall (facing page top), which runs from Tyne to Solway, undeterred by crag or precipice, and which admits no interruption. Even after centuries of decay and desolation it is impossible not to look at the work and marvel.

Travelling north from Newcastle over the Roman Wall, the scenery of the ancient Kingdom of Northumbria is wild and solitary. Following the broad tide line of the dune-girt shore, the Castle of Bamburgh (facing page bottom) is eventually reached. Here is the strongest of a chain of stone fortifications strung across the Scottish borderlands.

In Scotland's southern lands a soft, poetic light informs scenes of a picturesque splendour with a strange and irrepressible charm – such as that which surrounds Sir Walter Scott's country house (facing page) at Abbotsford, in a wooded setting close to the banks of the author's beloved River Tweed. Abbotsford was the last, and is certainly the most famous, of the author's homes, and it was here that he died in 1832.

The whole of the Lowlands seem touched by the spirit of Sir Walter Scott's historical romances, for the countryside appears everywhere to be dominated by its past and studded with medieval remains, such as the bare ruins of Dryburgh Abbey (below). Here, in the abbey's St Mary's Aisle, is the burial place of Sir Walter and members of his family, as well as that of J.G. Lockhart, his biographer, and Field Marshal Earl Haig.

'Edina! Scotia's darling seat!/All hail thy palaces and tow'rs, …/There Architecture's noble pride/Bids elegance and splendour rise'. Robert Burns knew the beautiful city of Edinburgh (above) well, and he is but one of the many poets and ballad writers moved to praise the Scottish capital. A short distance to the west of Edinburgh are the two great bridges (left) of the Forth estuary. The cantilever Forth Bridge, built in the 19th century, is used exclusively for railway traffic, while the New Forth Bridge serves road transport.

Off the coast, to the northeast of North Berwick, lies Bass Rock (left). Known primarily for its lighthouse, it was once a prison for Covenanters, and it also has associations with Robert Louis Stevenson's *Catriona*. Now seabirds inhabit the rock in their thousands. The isles of the Western Coast possess a beauty which is all their own; an effect of light playing on the sea. Inshore the water is vivid blue, or even turquoise where the yellow of the shore changes the sea's hue, as seen at Baile Mor (facing page), on St Columba's Iona. As the sea recedes from the shore, so its depth changes its colour to a deep violet, or an indigo sheen.

Standing ten miles offshore from Girvan, in Ayrshire, is the lonely, domed granite rock known as Ailsa Craig (facing page), whose precipitous cliffs and fissures – thronged with screaming seabirds – perfectly conveys the rugged atmosphere of the rugged coastline of this part of Scotland.

A glance at the map of Scotland reveals how endlessly freshwater lochs stud the region, and how fantastically indented by the sea is the coastline, as at Rhunahaorine Point (below), on Kintyre. Tortuous kyles and sea lochs add to the scenic effect, allowing the sea to send its groping fingers amid the mountains.

Culzean Castle (facing page top) stands on the Strathclyde coast, and is a typical product of the 18th-century Picturesque style – a building of Georgian symmetry and order, but with medieval trimmings. Before its renovation the house was known simply as *'The Cove',* but finding that a grandson of the first owner of the castle, John Kennedy, had styled himself *'Joannes Kennedy de Culzane'* in 1492, it was written *Culzean* in the parish records, and Culzean it became.

Set in Glasgow's Kelvingrove Park is the imposing Gothic fantasy of the Art Gallery and Museum (facing page bottom).

At Gigha Island (right) the view is westward across the Sound of Jura to distant Islay.

Realising that her heart was in the Highlands, Queen Victoria resolved to make a home at Balmoral. The Prince Consort therefore purchased the estate in 1852 for £31,000 and had the old house rebuilt in his own version of the Scottish Baronial style. The resultant chateau-like mansion of Balmoral Castle (left) is rich in 'fairy story' turrets and gables. Lying on a large, sweeping curve of the River Dee, it is surrounded by pine woods, heather moors and sombre expanses of deer forest.

Tobermory (facing page), 'The Well of Mary', is the chief town on the Island of Mull. It was founded in 1788 by the Society for the Encouragement of the British Fisheries, but failed to realise the hopes of its founders and has never been an important fishing station.

The deep and changing colours of the seas around the Western Isles of Scotland throw into sharp contrast the white sand bars of Scaraster Bay (left) on South Harris. Further south, off the Cowal coast, and separated from it by the lovely Kyles of Bute, is the equally lovely Isle of Bute (below). The island itself is about fifteen miles long, and averages some three to five miles across, with the resort of Rothesay a major attraction.

Sited at the confluence of the rivers Leven and Clyde, Dumbarton (facing page) was once the centre of the independent Kingdom of Strathclyde, and it has a royal castle standing on the majestic, 240ft-high Dumbarton Rock. To the west is the port of Tarbert (right), the centre of the Loch Fyne herring industry. Tarbert lies on the tiny isthmus on the shores of East Loch Tarbert – the little neck of land linking Knapdale with Kintyre. Magnus Barefoot of Norway is said to have been ceremonially dragged by his warriors in a longship from Tarbert across this isthmus, a distance of nearly two miles, in 1093.

Rothesay (facing page) has given its name to the Prince of Wales' dukedom and, sited on sandy Rothesay Bay, it is the principal town of the Isle of Bute. The harbour is full of small craft in July, when the Clyde Yachting Fortnight is in full swing and steamers call at the pier. Behind the pier is Rothesay Castle which, when seen from above, stands out from the town as a green square with a moated fortress at its centre.

The old University town of St Andrews (below) has several claims to fame. It boasts the most celebrated golf course in the world, and is the home of the Royal and Ancient Golf Club, which was founded in 1754 and is not only world famed, but is also the acknowledged ruling authority on the game. The university itself is the oldest in Scotland. It was founded in 1412 and once included Dundee University.

For many people St Andrews (facing page) means nothing but golf, for its incomparable links make it a mecca for followers of the 'Royal and Ancient Game'. However, St Andrews was once also the spiritual centre of Scotland, though its cathedral now lies in ruins.

Much of Dundee (above), Scotland's fourth largest city, lying on the north bank of the Firth of Tay, is modern. It became a Royal Burgh, however, as long ago as 1190, and at various times endured considerable suffering during wars with the English.

The famed Gleneagles Hotel (left), and the noted golf course of the same name, one of the best-known in Scotland, is set in the green and bronze moorland landscape near the village of Auchterarder, between Strath Allan and Strath Earn.

It does not take the road at Glen Shee (below) long to rise out of its vale to the surrounding high country of the mountains. As at mist-shrouded Loch Tay (facing page), it is not a comfortable scene that meets the eye, but one to marvel at in all its threatening majesty.

The gaunt and towering fortress of Stirling Castle (facing page), where both James II and James V were born, looks out from its rocky pinnacle over the greatest field of Scottish valour, Bannockburn, where Robert Bruce achieved Scottish independence when he defeated the English armies under Edward II in 1314. The soul of the Highlands lies in the heather-capped mountain heights far above the ordinary haunts of men. The very names of some of them have a quality of godlike mystery and grandeur, even of terror – Stobinian, Lochnagar, and dark Schiehallion (right), which rises for 3,547ft above Loch Rannoch, and is one of the best-known landmarks in the Central Highlands.

The waters of Loch Ness are darkened by peaty soil brought down to the waters by the numerous small burns and rivers that feed it. The murky depths are reputedly the haunt of its famous monster, stories of which stretch back to the 6th century – when St Columba is said to have prevented it from eating a Pict – and beyond, into the mists of Gaelic lore, which states that an *each Visque*, or fearsome water-horse, inhabits every dark sheet of water in the Highlands.

Loch Ness is one of a chain of lochs lying in Glen More, also known as the 'Great Glen of Alban', or more usually simply as the Great Glen, a remarkable geographical feature, virtually separating the mainland of Scotland into two parts. Loch Ness extends from south of Inverness (facing page), popularly dubbed 'The Capital of the Highlands', to Fort Augustus (below), where the twin courses of the Caledonian Canal empty into the southern extremity of the loch.

Queen's View (above), Perth, is a famous outlook on the
north bank of the River Tummel, a little to the east of the
loch itself. From the viewpoint may be seen the river, the
loch and a sweep of mountains in all their beauty; all of
which was certainly visited, and presumably enjoyed, by
Queen Victoria in 1866.